W9-CED-993

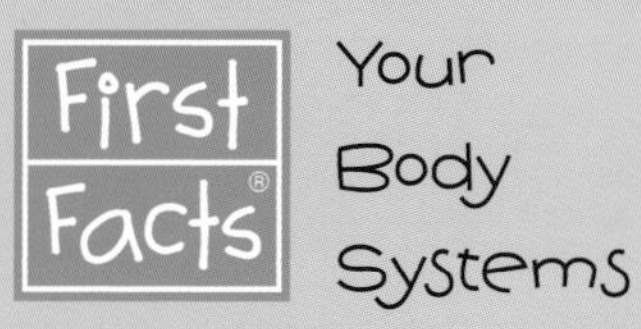

Your Respiratory System Works!

by Flora Brett

CAPSTONE PRESS
a capstone imprint

First Facts are published by Capstone Press,
1710 Roe Crest Drive, North Mankato, Minnesota 56003
www.capstonepub.com

Library of Congress Cataloging-in-Publication Data
Brett, Flora, author.
Your respiratory system works! / by Flora Brett.
pages cm. — (First facts. Your body systems)
Summary: "Engaging text and imformative images help readers learn about their respiratory system"— Provided by publisher.
Audience: Ages 6–9.
Audience: K to grade 3.
Includes bibliographical references and index.
ISBN 978-1-4914-2067-6 (library binding) — ISBN 978-1-4914-2251-9 (pbk.) —
ISBN 978-1-4914-2273-1 (ebook PDF)
1. Respiratory organs—Juvenile literature. 2. Cardiopulmonary system—Juvenile literature. 3. Lungs—Juvenile literature. 4. Human physiology—Juvenile literature. [1. Respiratory system.] I. Title.
QP121.B827 2015
612.2—dc23
2014023834

Editorial Credits
Emily Raij and Nikki Bruno Clapper, editors; Cynthia Akiyoshi, designer; Svetlana Zhurkin, media researcher; Laura Manthe, production specialist

Photo Credits
Capstone, 9; Shutterstock: Alila Medical Media, 5, AntiMartina (dotted background), cover and throughout, ecade3d, 11, Gert Very, 7, Jacek Chabraszewski, 20, Lightspring, 15, Maya2008, cover, 1, Michael C. Gray, 17, Serhiy Kobyakov, cover (top right), back cover, 1 (top right), 19, Simone van den Berg, 13, Stuart Monk, 21

Printed in the United States of America in North Mankato, Minnesota.
092014 008482CGS15

Table of Contents

Breathing and Blowing

Your respiratory system is always in motion. It works when you blow bubbles, talk to a friend, or sleep.

The respiratory system includes your lungs, airways, and **respiration** muscles. This system works with your other body systems. It helps keep your body healthy and active. Without your respiration system, you couldn't breathe!

Fact:

Your lungs breathe in more than 2,100 gallons (7,950 liters) of air every day.

respiration—the process of taking in oxygen and sending out carbon dioxide

The Respiratory System

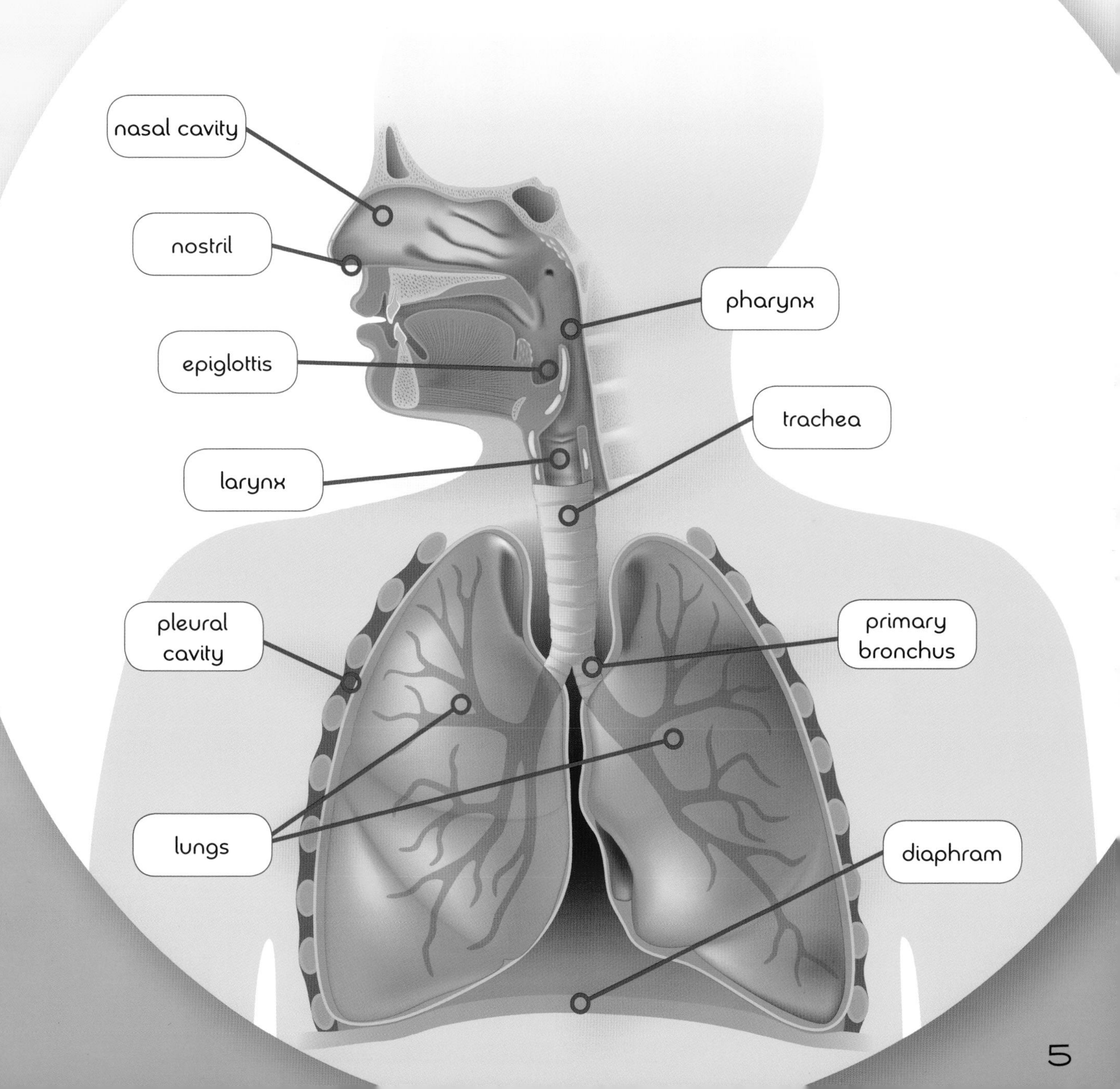

Gases In and Out

Your body needs a gas called oxygen to live. The cells in your body get energy from oxygen and food.

When you breathe in, air carries oxygen into your body. When you breathe out, your body gets rid of carbon dioxide. Carbon dioxide is a gas that your cells give off as waste. Too much carbon dioxide is poisonous to the body.

Fact:

You can't live for more than a few minutes without oxygen.

A swimmer fuels up with new oxygen.

When You Take a Breath

When you breathe in, air enters your nose or mouth. From your nose, air travels to the nasal cavity. This is a little cave behind your nose. Here the air gets warmed, moistened, and cleaned before it travels to the lungs.

Hairs in the nose trap dirt from the air. In the nasal cavity, a thick liquid called **mucus** traps more germs and dust. Tiny hairs called **cilia** line the nasal cavity. Cilia keep mucus moving toward your nose and mouth. You sneeze or cough out the mucus.

Fact:

Healthy nose cilia move back and forth 14 to 16 times per second.

body parts involved in breathing

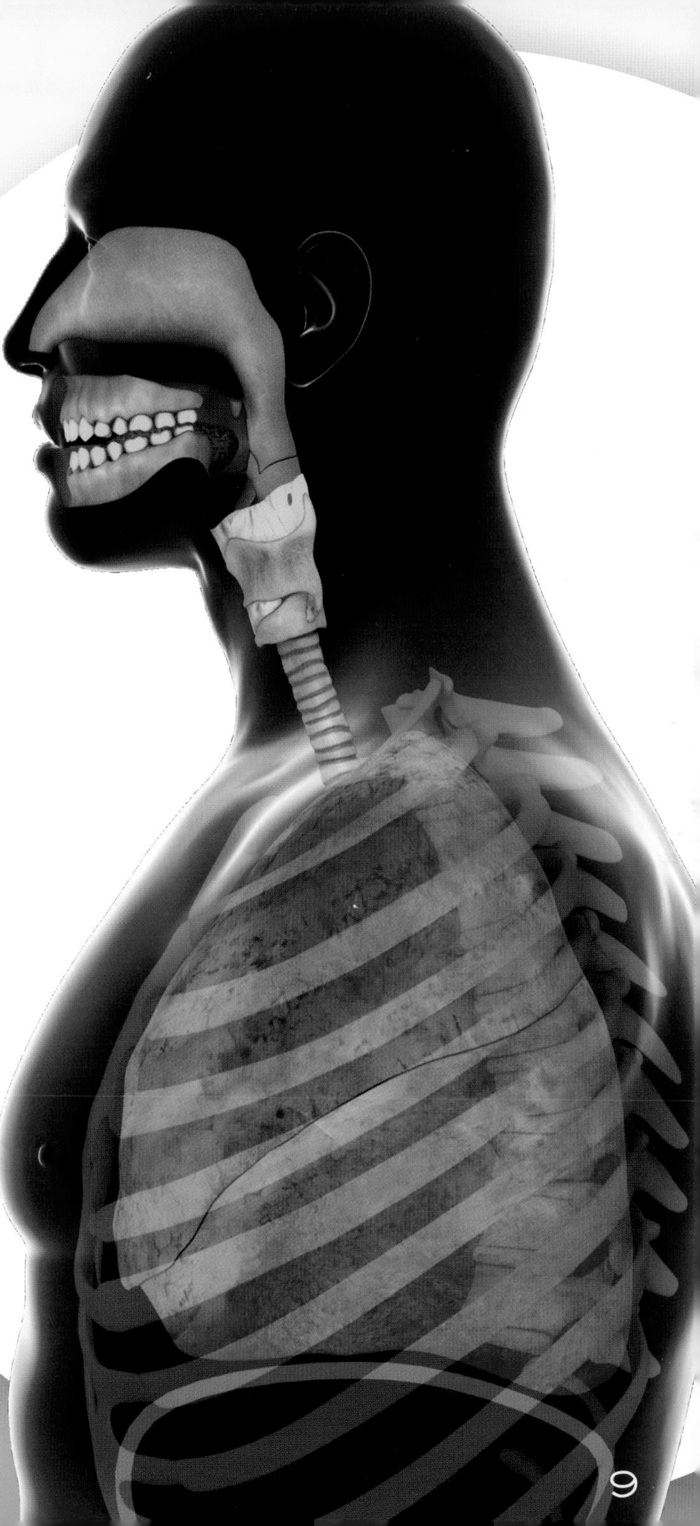

mucus—a slimy liquid that coats the inside of a person's breathing passages

cilia—short hairs that line the nasal cavity

Getting to the Lungs

Next, air travels down the throat to the **larynx**, or voice box. Your larynx holds your **vocal cords**. You use these to talk.

Then air flows through a tube called the **trachea**. The bottom of the trachea splits into two airways. These airways carry air to the two lungs. Air travels through smaller airways in the lungs. Then it reaches tiny air sacs called alveoli. Oxygen passes through the walls of the alveoli and into the blood.

larynx—the upper part of the trachea that holds the vocal cords

vocal cords—bands of skin in a person's air pipe; air from the lungs passes through the vocal cords; this causes the vocal cords to vibrate and make sound

trachea—the air passage that connects the nose and the mouth to the lungs

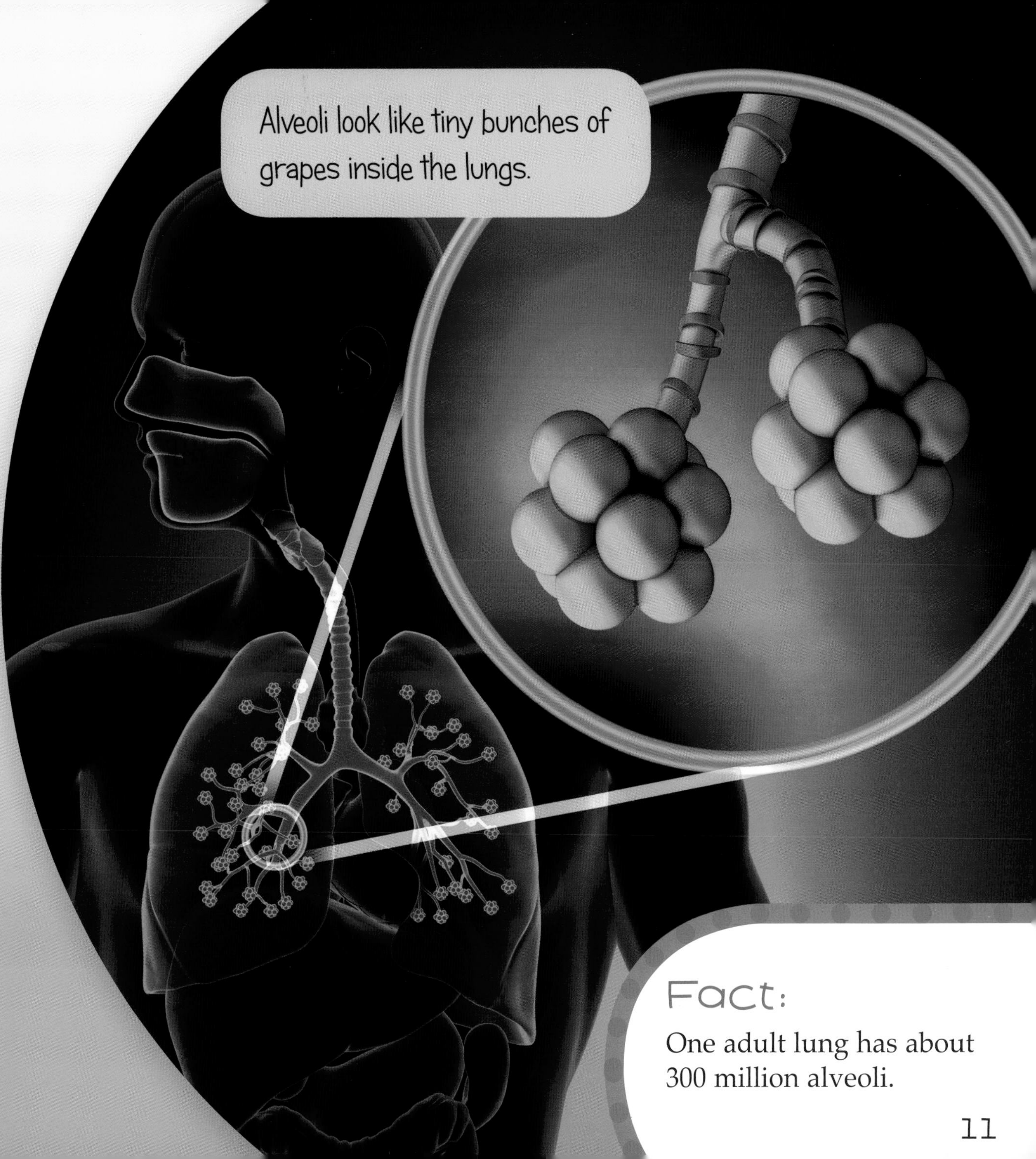

Alveoli look like tiny bunches of grapes inside the lungs.

Fact:

One adult lung has about 300 million alveoli.

Lungs and Diaphragm

Take a deep breath in. Your **diaphragm** muscle pulls your lungs down. At the same time, your rib muscles push your chest out. These actions let your lungs get bigger as they fill with air.

When you breathe out, your diaphragm, rib, and chest muscles relax. Your lungs shrink as air is pushed out of them.

diaphragm—the muscle under your lungs that moves when you breathe

Fact:

Hiccups are sudden movements of the diaphragm.

Lungs and Heart

The lungs and the heart trade gases at the alveoli. The heart pumps blood through blood vessels. Small blood vessels called **capillaries** surround the lungs' alveoli. Oxygen travels from the alveoli into the capillaries.

Blood carries oxygen to the heart and then throughout the body. Blood also carries carbon dioxide to the heart. Your heart pumps blood filled with carbon dioxide back to the alveoli. Carbon dioxide leaves your lungs when you breathe out.

capillary—a small tube in your body that carries blood between the arteries and veins

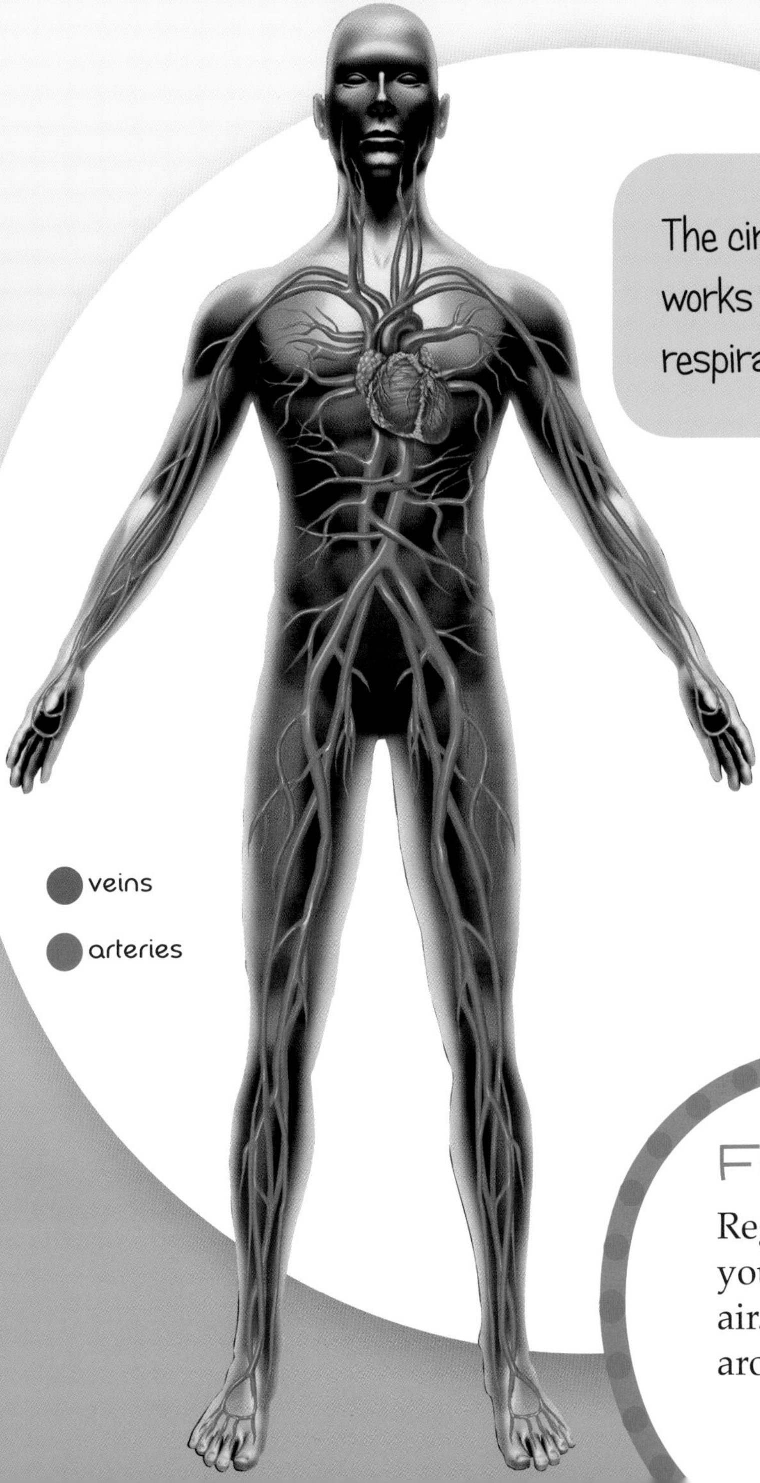

The circulatory system works together with the respiratory system.

veins

arteries

Fact:

Regular exercise helps your lungs hold more air. Then oxygen moves around your body faster.

Using Your Voice

The larynx, vocal cords, and mouth help you make sounds. Vocal cords stretch across an opening in the larynx. When you speak, air moves from your lungs across your vocal cords. The cords move and make sound waves that travel out of your mouth.

You tighten muscles in your vocal cords to make high-pitched sounds. You loosen your vocal-cord muscles to make low-pitched sounds. Mouth and throat muscles help you make more sounds.

Fact:

Every person's voice sounds different. Two reasons for these differences are vocal-cord length and larynx size.

Respiratory Problems

Most people have respiratory infections now and then. Do you ever have a sore throat? Do you feel extra mucus in your throat or nose? If so, you probably have a cold. You get rid of extra mucus by coughing or blowing it out.

Allergies also cause extra mucus, sneezing, and watery eyes. Swollen nasal passages and coughing can make it harder to breathe.

Fact:

Asthma is a respiratory disease. It causes the airways to swell and fill with mucus. This can make breathing extremely difficult.

allergy—a reaction to something that doesn't cause a reaction in most people, such as foods, pets, or dust

asthma—a lung disease that can make it hard to breathe

Keeping Lungs Healthy

You can help keep your respiratory system healthy. First, stop germs from entering your body. Wash your hands often. Also, keep your hands away from your mouth and nose.

Second, do not smoke. Smoking tobacco damages cells in your lungs. It can cause diseased cells to replace healthy cells. It's important to keep your lungs free of smoke and pollution.

Amazing but True!

Have you ever wondered why you yawn? Nobody knows! Some scientists think that yawning helps cool your body. When you are sleepy, your body temperature is slightly higher than usual. Yawns help cool you down.

Glossary

allergy (AL-lur-gee)—a reaction to something that doesn't cause a reaction in most people, such as foods, pets, or dust

asthma (AZ-muh)—a lung disease that can make it hard to breathe

capillary (KAP-uh-ler-ee)—a small tube in your body that carries blood between the arteries and veins

cilia (SIL-ee-uh)—short hairs that line the nasal cavity

diaphragm (DIE-uh-fram)—the muscle under the lungs that moves when you breathe

larynx (LA-ringks)—the upper part of the trachea that holds the vocal cords

mucus (MYOO-kuhs)—a slimy liquid that coats the inside of a person's breathing passages

respiration (ress-puh-RAY-shuhn)—the process of taking in oxygen and sending out carbon dioxide

trachea (TRAY-kee-uh)—the air passage that connects the nose and the mouth to the lungs

vocal cords (VOH-kuhl KORDS)—bands of skin in a person's air pipe; air from the lungs passes through the vocal cords; this causes the vocal cords to vibrate and make sound

Read More

Jango-Cohen, Judith. *Your Respiratory System.* Searchlight Books: How Does Your Body Work? Minneapolis: Lerner Publications Co., 2013.

Reina, Mary. *A Tour of Your Respiratory System.* First Graphics: Body Systems. North Mankato, Minn.: Capstone Press, 2013.

Taylor, Lauren. *My Lively Heart and Lungs.* Inside Me. Mankato, Minn.: QEB Pub., 2013.

Internet Sites

FactHound offers a safe, fun way to find Internet sites related to this book. All of the sites on FactHound have been researched by our staff.

Here's all you do:
Visit *www.facthound.com*
Type in this code: 9781491420676

Check out projects, games and lots more at **www.capstonekids.com**

Critical Thinking Using the Common Core

1. How does oxygen move through your body? How does carbon dioxide get pushed out? (Key Ideas and Details)
2. Think about how smoking can damage a person's respiratory system. What facts could you use to convince someone to quit smoking? (Integration of Knowledge and Ideas)
3. Explain one reason why people might yawn. (Key Ideas and Details)

Index